> **"As long as there is breath in your body, there is hope!"**
>
> --Rosalind Y. Tompkins

AS LONG AS THERE IS BREATH IN YOUR BODY, THERE IS HOPE

A Gripping Tale of a Woman's Journey through the Hell-Hole of Addiction into Abundant Life

Rosalind Y. Tompkins

Scripture quotations marked KJV are from the King James
Version of the Holy Bible.
Scripture quotations marked NIV are from the New
International Version of the Holy Bible.
Used by permission.

AS LONG AS THERE IS BREATH IN YOUR BODY, THERE IS HOPE

Cover design by Lisa Corp

Printed in the United States of America

ISBN 0-9747439-0-9

Contents

Page

Acknowledgments iii

Foreword v

Prologue vii

<u>ACT I</u>
Chapter
1   A LIFE WORTH LIVING 1
2   TO HELL 5
3   BACK FROM HELL 15
4   CRACK HELL 23
5   WHEN HELL FREEZES OVER ... 31
6   ABUNDANT LIFE BEGINS 43

<u>ACT II</u>
Chapter
7   PEARLS OF WISDOM 69
8   I AM LOVE 73

Chapter		Page
9	I PRAY	83
10	I AM RESILIENT	97
11	I AM HOPE	105
12	I AM UNITY	115
13	I AM HUMBLE	147
14	I AM PASSION	155
15	I AM VALUABLE	163
	Epilogue	171
	Testimonial	173
	Works Cited	175
	About the Author	177

Acknowledgments

This book is dedicated to all of the women who have lost their lives battling drug addiction. It is also dedicated to all of the women who are yet struggling. Don't give up because there is hope as long as there is breath in your body!

I want to thank the Lord Jesus Christ, my mother, Louise Clark, my daughter, Janar Tompkins, and the Mothers In Crisis leadership team who labor endlessly in the vineyard with me day after day. A special thanks goes out to Liz Delancy for her help in this particular endeavor. I thank God for my Bishop, Dr. Mark J. Chironna for all of the inspiration and

AS LONG AS THERE IS BREATH...

encouragement that propels me to reach for higher.

Foreword

BROKENNESS—reduced to fragments; fragmented; ruptured; torn; fractured; weakened in strength, spirit, etc. tamed, trained, or reduced to submission, i.e., "my life"

Webster's Encyclopedic Unabridged Dictionary of the English Language New Revised Edition

Prologue

Dear Beloved,

This is a book about my life experiences and the life experiences of others who have battled drug and alcohol addiction. Everyone has a story to tell. *As Long As There Is Breath in Your Body, There Is Hope*, is a part of my life story. It is a collage of experiences that forms bits and pieces of the big picture of my life. In *Act I* of the book I share parts of my life experiences that led to brokenness. They were extremely difficult times for me, but I share them in love in order to inspire hope. No man is an island. We need each other. It is through sharing that we connect one to another. In **Act II** of the book I share life lessons that I call "pearls of wisdom" that I learned along the way. The life experiences shared during **Act II** are presented as they relate to a particular topic and are not necessarily in chronological order. They are shared to help illustrate a point.

As Long As There Is Breath in Your Body, There Is Hope, is my way of connecting with you. I can reach out and touch you by sharing a glimpse of my path to brokenness and "pearls of wisdom" gathered on the journey. I share a lot about the ministry of **Mothers In Crisis**, my "baby of hope" that was birthed out of the pain that I went through. It's always good when you can get something for all of your trouble. **Mothers In Crisis** is my something.

Many years ago someone said to me that I had a marketable testimony. I couldn't relate because no amount of compensation can recompense for the pain and suffering that I went through. Today as I share some of the painful events of my life it is not for gain but for glory. I share my testimony for God to be glorified for what He has done in my life and the lives of others. Whatever is gained will be used for the up building of His kingdom and for His glory. "To God Be the Glory"!

I pray that as you read *As Long As There Is Breath in Your Body, There Is Hope* you will be inspired in your own recovery whether it is from drugs and alcohol or other challenges that we all face in life. As I share the experiences of others, some names have been changed in order to protect confidentiality.

With Love,

Rosalind Y. Tompkins

ACT I

1

A LIFE WORTH LIVING

Let me ask you a question. Are you breathing? You might say, "Well that is obvious." But not so fast, when I ask the question, are you breathing? I am referring to life. Life in terms of what the Bible refers to as abundant life. Not just merely existing, but truly living and doing it with peace, love, and joy. It's impossible to do that when you are addicted to alcohol and other drugs. Addiction robs abundant life and reduces an addicted

1

person to merely existing. Over the course of time, I have met thousands of people whose lives were ripped apart by the "hell-hole of addiction," reduced to merely existing. I was one of those people. I spent twelve years addicted to various drugs. I started using marijuana when I was twelve years old. My addiction progressed until I was a full-blown crack-cocaine addict by the age of twenty-two. By the grace of God, I was able to turn a hopeless, desperate situation into a place of hope. My journey to hope began at the place of desperation.

Hopeless people are desperate people. The question is what do you do with the desperation? The answer is, there are many things that you can do, but only one-thing matters and that is to allow the desperation to lead to brokenness. Brokenness leads to searching for answers other than the ones that have been tried before. That's what happened to me on my journey to brokenness. I had to try something different and take another path. The path that I was on was leading me nowhere but down real fast. Can you relate?

THE LAST WORD

"The thief cometh not, but for to steal, and kill, and to destroy: I am come that they might have life, and that they might have it more abundantly."
JOHN 10:10 (KJV)

2

TO HELL

My path to brokenness began when I was nineteen years old. I was a sophomore at Florida State University and my daily diet consisted of drugs and alcohol. I had spent my young life partying and getting high as often as I could. I wasn't thinking about my health, exercising, or eating right. The break came one day when I was home alone in my apartment. I can remember it as though it were yesterday. It was dry in terms of not being able to get any drugs. My roommate had gone out with a friend in order to try to find some. I was standing in the bathroom, looking in the mirror, talking to myself. It wasn't as though I talked to myself often; it was just that I wasn't used to being alone. I always had my roommate or someone else with me at all times. However that night I was all alone, when all of a sudden it was like something or someone entered my body and my eyes became filled with tears and my thoughts began to race with several rituals popping into my mind at an alarming rate. By rituals I mean my mind was telling me that if I did this, that would happen, or if I did that, then this would happen. It was stupid stuff like if you squeeze your thighs together that would cause something to happen that was not in the least bit related. I had never experienced anything like this even while taking hallucinogenic drugs. The conversation in my head was supposedly about God. God was saying this and God was saying that.

When my roommate finally came home she took one look at me and asked me what in the hell had happened to me. Years later, I realize that hell had just happened to me indeed! At the time however, I told her that I had an experience with God. She just looked at me strange and asked me where the drugs were that I had been smoking. I am convinced that hell begins in the mind. If it is true that the mind is the battlefield then I was desperately losing the battle.

This all took place during my Christmas break from Florida State University in 1982. My roommate and I were supposed to go to Germany to visit her parents for the holidays. We had the tickets, passports and everything. Fortunately, we had to go to my home in Pensacola, Florida first. I say fortunately because it was in Pensacola that I totally lost touch with reality and had to be hospitalized because my erratic behavior had become increasingly worse. I had begun staring at people I didn't know and I continued to hear that conversation in my head telling me to do this and that would happen, do that and this would happen, etc. I was committed into a psychiatric hospital by my mother and stepfather. What a let down that was, instead of going to Germany for Christmas, I was in the mental ward! While there, I was given all kinds of medication that made me stiff in my joints and drool out of the side of my mouth. Through all of this I was somehow convinced that there was nothing wrong with me. I thought everybody else was the problem, like my mother, my roommate, the man walking down the street, anybody but me. I had become quite paranoid. The doctors weren't sure why I was acting the way I was because I had no history of mental illness and there were no drugs in my system at the time of hospitalization. They were able to determine that I was an addict through the initial psychosocial interview; therefore their diagnosis was that I was experiencing a flash back because of the hallucinogenic drug ("mushroom tea") that I drank all summer. I must add that I was also daily using cocaine, marijuana, and drinking. For a long time I was very angry about the fact that my roommate used the same drugs but she didn't have a mental break down. I couldn't understand why she was able to go to Germany while I was locked up in a psychiatric ward. The explanation that my roommate gave was that I was weak and of course she was strong. I was angry with her mainly because I believed that I was weak and if I could have some how handled it, I wouldn't have lost it. At the same time, my roommate also believed that I was faking. Needless to say our friendship did not survive the strain of my mental breakdown.

Over the course of the next two years I was in and out of psychiatric hospitals on four different occasions. The worse incident occurred in Miami, Florida when I went to stay with my brother and his wife. Upon release from the mental ward in Pensacola, I had insisted that I be allowed to go and live with my brother in Miami. My mother was against that idea and it turned out to be for a very good reason. In fact that was one of the worst things that I could have done because I continued to smoke marijuana and snort cocaine daily. I lost touch with reality again after about a month in Miami and began to scream uncontrollably. I was taken to Jackson Memorial hospital in the back of a police car. I quieted down while in the police car but the moment I entered the waiting room of Jackson Memorial I began to scream at the people who were there. I was immediately rushed into the back and strapped down with my hands cuffed to a bed. I felt like a trapped animal.

I hallucinated all night long that first night. I saw snakes and hollered in a loud voice. The next day hospital staff put me in a padded locked room in the back of the hospital so that I would not disturb anyone or hurt myself because I had begun banging my head on the walls. The only thing in that padded cell was a bed. I felt like a wild animal, my thoughts were racing, and I began to crawl around on my hands and knees. I tore up the bed, taking the sheets off and throwing them across the room. After stripping the bed I defecated in the middle. I was always in a wheel chair with one of my hands cuffed to the chair when they took me from my padded cell. I was totally out of control. I will never forget the feelings of total powerlessness and hopelessness that I felt. It was like being outside of myself and into a monster.

THE LAST WORD

"For though we walk in the flesh, we do not war after the flesh: (For the weapons of our warfare are not carnal, but mighty through God to the pulling down of strong holds;) Casting down imaginations, and every high thing that exalteth itself against the knowledge of God, and bringing into captivity every thought to the obedience of Christ."
2 CORINTHIANS 10:3-5 (KJV)

3

BACK FROM HELL

While I was out of my mind and totally out of control in Jackson Memorial Hospital's psychiatric ward, one of my first cousins was hit by a car in Miami. My mother and my aunt rushed to Miami from Pensacola to see about their children. It was a trying time indeed.

When my mother first came to see me in Jackson Memorial I didn't even recognize her. I thought she was my sister. I was in such a psychotic state; I didn't know my head from my toes for a solid week. The turning point came when my mother, aunt, sister, cousins, and other family members came and prayed for me at the hospital. I was still in such bad condition that they had to roll me into the day room in a wheel chair. I was strapped to the chair and drooling. My mother asked me if I recognized my family members. I began to name each person. It was as though for that brief moment I was in touch with reality. We joined hands as a family and began to pray. After that particular visit, I began to miraculously regain reality and some sense of control. I felt like a human being again. After that day, I was finally taken from the padded locked room in the back of the hospital and put with the rest of the patients on the ward.

While on the ward with the rest of the patients I had to sleep with my shoes under my pillow or I would wake up to see other patients wearing them. As I began to regain my senses, I realized the condition that I had been in and the place that I was in and it wasn't a pretty picture. I felt tremendous shame and guilt. Being in the hospital, felt like being in a zoo for human beings. We were animals who had to be corralled into submission through medication and other means such as restraints. As I continued to regain my ability to think clearly my mother prepared to take me home with her to Pensacola. I am so glad that I was more in touch with reality at this time because on one occasion I remember a male attendant waking me up in the middle of the night and taking me to a back room. The same padded cell where I had spent the first week. He took me into the cell and closed the door. I had sense enough to wonder why I was being taken back to that room in the middle of the night because I wasn't hollering or banging my head or anything, I was asleep. To my horror and profound dismay he unzipped his pants and attempted to make me perform oral sex on him. I just kept my mouth closed and shook my head until he took me back to my room. I thank God that he didn't force me. I didn't tell my family or hospital staff about what happened to me because after all, I was the one institutionalized for bizarre behavior but I must say that I wasn't the crazy one in this instance! I chose to block the memory of what happened that night out of my mind and I didn't think about it until years later.

The hospital psychiatrists and staff had a hard time ascertaining exactly why I had the mental breakdown. They attributed it to the drugs that I had been taking and said that I would need to be on medication for the rest of my life because of a chemical imbalance that had taken place. I was eventually discharged and went home to Pensacola with my mother. The hospital gave her pills for me to take. They stated that they were nerve pills and I would have to take them for the rest of my life. However that wasn't the case. We threw those pills in the trash on the way out of the hospital. I never took them again because through prayer God gave me my mind back!

Through the experiences of losing my mind I was broken to a certain degree. I began to realize that I wasn't invincible. I even decided to make a few changes in my life. However I still didn't make the connection between my rebellious ways and my pain. I still had too much of me in me. I believed that I had a right to do what I wanted to do when I wanted to do it. I believed that I just couldn't take certain kinds of drugs but others were okay for me to continue to consume.

THE LAST WORD

"If the Son therefore shall make you free, ye shall be free indeed."
JOHN 8:36 (KJV)

4

CRACK HELL

I eventually moved back to Tallahassee to attend Florida State University. You would think that I would have learned to stay away from drugs and alcohol because of what I had gone through, but that wasn't the case. I was convinced that it was just the hallucinogenic drugs that I needed to stay away from. Everything else was fair game. Therefore, I continued to smoke marijuana, snort cocaine, and drink alcohol. I stayed away from the mushroom tea and all hallucinogenic drugs though. It was just the grace of God that kept me from losing my mind again. It certainly wasn't because of my lifestyle.

A supposedly "new" drug hit the streets and I was there to meet it. It really wasn't a new drug, just a different form of an old drug. I am referring to free base cocaine. Freebasing was simply cooking the cocaine with baking soda until it became hard and then smoking it with a pipe. Free base cocaine was the same drug that comedian Richard Prior was smoking when he caught on fire! It was a very dangerous drug that appeared harmless.

My friends and I would free base for hours

because you couldn't sleep while doing the drug. I thought I was in heaven on many occasions. I didn't realize that I had made my way back to hell until this drug form of freebasing was taken to another level and became crack-cocaine. All of sudden the drug came pre-packaged in God only knows what. It was sold in rock form and was relatively cheap in comparison to powder cocaine. I have never experienced a high as demonic as the crack-cocaine high. It is demanding and consuming. The crack-cocaine high is seductive and destructive all at the same time. While smoking crack-cocaine, I would receive a rush instantaneously, in about 8 seconds, and then continue to smoke rock after rock trying to experience the initial rush. It never came. The high drove me to continue using at all cost. It was cheap to buy, but the price was high in terms of costing my self-respect and the life of my unborn child. The nature of the high will cause you to do whatever it takes in order to get the drug. I've known people to sell everything in their house, including the food in the refrigerator in order to get another hit. If I could not continue to get high, my body would ache all over and I couldn't sleep or concentrate on doing anything else until about five or six hours later.

I got pregnant while exchanging sex for

drugs. I realized once I became clean and sober that it was a stupid thing to do, but at the time I was hopelessly addicted to crack-cocaine and I had to have the drug no matter what. I didn't even remember the man's name, but I ended up carrying his child. I tried to stop using drugs while I was pregnant, but I couldn't completely. For the most part, I stopped using crack-cocaine, but I continued to smoke marijuana and snort powder cocaine occasionally. I also smoked cigarettes heavily. During my sixth month of pregnancy the baby gave up and stopped breathing. I had to deliver her still born. While delivering my dead baby, I experienced the pain of labor because the doctors had to induce labor. I had my baby through natural childbirth; the only problem was, after delivery I couldn't hear her cry. I named her Janadra Elizabeth Tompkins. I finally began to realize that life was not a joke; life wasn't just one big party with fun and games. I wasn't laughing; as a matter of fact I was crying because it hurt like hell. I remember writing in my journal, "Why God? There has to be a reason for going through all of this pain." I found out later in life what that reason was. I can truly say the brokenness that I experienced at that time in my life was not of the mind but of the heart and there is a big difference. The only problem was, the brokenness of the spirit was still more life experiences away.

THE LAST WORD

"There is a way that seems right to a man, but in the end it leads to death."
PROVERBS 14:12 (NIV)

/

5

WHEN HELL FREEZES OVER

I guess the saying, "there is no place like home" was true for me because after the loss of my baby girl, I went to stay with my mother and stepfather once again in Pensacola. During that period of my life, I was quite depressed. All I did was lie around the house, look at television, eat, and think. I thought long and hard about my life as I recuperated from the loss of my baby. My mother lived near the Pensacola Bay and there was a park on the water that I would go to everyday. I remember sitting and looking out at the water and thinking about where I would be in five years. I couldn't see anything. I saw nothing but darkness. I knew that I had to do something or I would die on the vine so to speak, so I decided to go back to Tallahassee to continue my education. I returned to Tallahassee much more sober in terms of life, but then again, I wasn't completely through with marijuana. I was deceived into believing that marijuana wasn't a problem. I told myself that after all it was just an herb grown by nature. I further justified my use by thinking that my troubles started when I used other drugs, but marijuana was okay. I had an image of myself smoking a joint while in a rocking chair as a grandmother on the back porch. I had no intentions of giving up the weed.

Back in Tallahassee, I attended Florida State University once again and I got a job in the mall doing surveys for a marketing company. I was very good at it and I worked all day walking around the mall getting people to participate. On one occasion, I was trying to get respondents for a malt liquor survey. The participants had to fit a certain profile that the company was targeting. They were mostly looking for young black men and so was I. I met this tall "milk chocolate" colored young man just sitting in the mall doing nothing. He looked as though he was just killing time. I approached him and asked him did he drink malt liquor and if he would like to participate in a survey. He said he did and would if I told him my name and telephone number. Needless to say, he participated and we began to talk. He told me that he was in Tallahassee by accident. He was enlisted in the Navy stationed in Jacksonville, FL. He and his friends were driving through this area on their way to somewhere else, when their car broke down in Gadsden County. It had to be towed to Tallahassee and he was just waiting for his friends to come back and pick him up. He said that they wouldn't be back until late that night.

I asked him if he would like to come to my apartment and wait for them because I lived right by the mall. He said of course and the rest is history. He began coming to see me as often as he could and I fell in love with him. I thought that I had finally found someone to live happily ever after with. For the first time, in a very long time, drugs were not the center of my life. I was still smoking marijuana, but I really was trying to do the right thing. I refused to have sex with him because I told him I was trying to turn my life around. He respected that for the most part, but we still would hug and kiss and even sleep in the same bed together.

One morning, I woke up in the act of making love. Somehow in the wee morning hours I gave in to temptation that was much too close to resist. Over the course of the relationship, which lasted about a year, we only made love that one time but that was all it took for me to get pregnant. He was out to sea when I found out I was pregnant. I really didn't want to be pregnant, but I thought that once he found out we would get married. I was very naïve. He never called or came back. I wrote him and called him to tell him about my pregnancy. He told me that he was already married and he didn't know why all these things were happening to him. I told him I didn't know what things were happening to him, but I knew what was happening to me, and I asked him what did he plan to do about it? He said that he would do what he could to take care of the baby and that was the last time I ever heard from him. I was devastated! I didn't know what to do. I talked to my boss at the marketing firm and she told me to continue to work. I did and for the first time in twelve long years, I stopped smoking marijuana. I actually stopped! It was hard. Some days after walking around the mall all day and finally going home to an empty apartment, I would lie on my bed and cry despairing unto death. I began to pray and read my Bible. I was mainly asking God to send my boyfriend back because my heart was broken. I was also asking the Lord for a healthy baby. I didn't want to go through what I went through with Janadra Elizabeth. That's why I stopped using drugs, alcohol and cigarettes altogether.

I made it through the nine months and had a healthy baby girl. I named her Janar Shenale Tompkins. Now I had to be responsible for someone other than myself. I made a conscious decision to breast feed Janar. I knew I couldn't use drugs and breast feed because the drugs would get into the baby's system through my milk. I was determined to remain drug free. It wasn't easy because after I had Janar my old friends started to come back around. On one occasion I visited a neighbor who I used to smoke marijuana with. I had Janar with me and we were all sitting around talking about my baby when my friends fired up a joint and began passing it around. When it came to me I was faced with a major decision. I knew that if I took a hit of that joint I would start back using regularly. Everything in me wanted to taste the weed that I had grown accustomed to for twelve years. All of a sudden when the joint came to me Janar began to cry. Her cry woke me up out of the trance like state that I had slipped into and I got my baby and left. I never visited that particular neighbor again.

In summary of the aforementioned events, I must say that after losing my mind on four different occasions, losing my self-respect, a child while on crack-cocaine, and ultimately losing the man I loved, my spirit was finally broken. I felt like a wild stallion that was finally tamed.

Out of my brokenness I began to search for answers and help in order to change my life. I had reached the end of my rope. I didn't know where to go, what to do, or who to call. I decided to call on Jesus. I surrendered my will to the will of the Lord Jesus Christ and I said to the Lord, "I give up." "Whatever you want me to do, I will do it." I fell on the *Rock* of my salvation!

THE LAST WORD

"Whosoever shall fall upon that stone shall be broken, but on whosoever it shall fall, it will grind him to powder..."
LUKE 20:18 (KJV)

6

ABUNDANT LIFE BEGINS

When Janar was about six months old I
decided that it was time to get a better job in
order to take care of my baby. I had continued
to work in the mall doing surveys and I also did
field work. It was a decent job but I knew that
as a single parent, I needed to make more
money. I had tried to find her father while I
was pregnant to no avail. I made a decision to
take care of Janar myself. After six long years
of ups and downs I finally graduated from

Florida State University with a Bachelors of Science Degree in Social Work.

The first job I got in my field of expertise was working at a residential drug treatment program. I only had one year clean! My job was a mental health technician on the midnight shift. I only made $4.75 and hour. It wasn't exactly what I had in mind but I felt that I could get my feet wet in the field of social work and then go after other jobs. I mainly babysat the clients at night and then went home to take care of Janar during the day. It was a time of transition in my life, and it wasn't easy. It seemed as though I never slept. I was happy though because I had my baby girl and I was still drug free. I also began to get a taste of what it felt like to help someone else. Prior to having Janar I was a very selfish person. It was all about me and what I wanted. Now I was beginning to think about others, starting with Janar and extending to the people who were in treatment, especially the women. I could identify with their issues because I had gone through much of what they were going through.

After working as a mental health technician for almost a year I was promoted to a newly formed position of an intervention specialist. It was a match made in heaven. The State of Florida was funding intervention specialists all across the state to deal with the problem of pregnant women using drugs, primarily crack-cocaine and having what they called "crack babies." Part of the roles and responsibilities of my new position included receiving referrals from various organizations such as the health departments, hospitals, the Department of Health and Rehabilitative Services known at that time as HRS, and others, identifying women who were in need of treatment. Often times the women were pregnant and using crack-cocaine, or either just had a baby born with cocaine in his or her system. I worked in both Leon and Gadsden Counties in Florida. I met many women during that era and oftentimes when I looked into their eyes I saw myself staring back at me. I remembered what hopelessness and despair felt like. I remembered the times that I was so out of it I didn't know my head from my toes and I really wanted to help them receive their recovery. The only problem was there was not much in the way of treatment opportunities available for pregnant and parenting women using drugs, especially in rural communities.

I began facilitating drug education support group meetings at a health department in Gadsden County and a neighborhood community center in Leon County. I used an agency van to pick up the women from their homes and bring them to the locations of the meetings.

I learned many things during this time period. I'll never forget the time I went to pick up a young lady from a housing project in an extremely drug infested rural community. The first thing that happened was that I had to literally dodge bullets to get to her apartment. Local police officers were chasing a drug dealer who began to shoot at them and of course they shot back. This was happening just as I was pulling up and getting out of the van. It clearly wasn't my day. The next thing that happened was the young lady that I went to pick up got on the van with a smoking hot "stem," i.e., drug paraphernalia in her hand. One of the other ladies saw it and told me. As I confronted the young lady I noticed that one of her hands was balled up in a tight fist. I asked her to open her hand and when she did the homemade pipe was there for the entire world to see, still hot from where she had just taken a hit. My first instinct was to demand that she get off the van. However, as I looked at her disheveled hair and clothes and her four children who were with her, I had compassion for her. As a result, I took the stem, told her and her children to sit down, and closed the door of the van. That day I drove to the meeting in tears. Today by the grace of God, that young lady is clean and sober.

One of the greatest lessons that I learned early on is the fact that everyone is responsible for their own recovery. No matter how much I may have wanted the women to get clean, or how much their families wanted them to get clean, or how much the government wanted them to get clean, they had to want to be clean and sober for themselves. That is what led me to the whole concept of empowerment.

Empowerment according to *Webster's Dictionary* is to be given power or authority to, to enable or permit. The women that I worked with needed to be given the power to get and stay clean. I believe that power is packaged in hope. To give hope is to give power. When the women began to see through my personal testimony, that recovery was possible and there was a way out, in many instances they grabbed hold of the "lifeline" of hope that was offered. I didn't agree with the concept of constantly declaring that, "my name is so and so, and I am an addict." I didn't agree with the concept of resolving oneself to powerlessness. I understood the need to first admit that you have a problem in order to break through denial. However, after that the women needed to be empowered to believe that they didn't have to remain an addict or powerless. That often included the need for more education, job skills, parenting skills, drug and alcohol counseling, housing assistance, love, support, encouragement, etc. I also knew from personal experience that the key to my ability to stay clean was my relationship with the Lord Jesus Christ.

After four years of working with this population I became intimately aware of what was available for women who were addicted to drugs and alcohol in the State of Florida and around the nation. It wasn't a pretty picture. Primarily the treatment programs were based upon a model of confrontation centered on the prototype of the "male alcoholic." Many treatment programs utilized methods that didn't value the women's genuine concern for the well

being of their babies. The women were often

told, "you weren't thinking about your baby

when you were on the streets." While that may

or may not have been the case, it was certainly a

valid issue that wasn't being addressed within

the treatments programs at that time. As a

result many women were leaving the residential

programs and not having successful outcomes

in their treatment attempts. I went to many

case staffings where professionals asked what

was wrong with these women that obviously

didn't want help? I began to ask the question,

"What is wrong with these treatment

programs?" During the late 1980's and early

1990's some counties in the State of Florida began prosecuting women who were using drugs while pregnant. The problem with that was even though the women were sentenced to treatment programs. If there were none available, they had to stay in jail until they had their babies. The response to drug addiction among women had become very punitive in nature. This deterred many women from seeking help.

In April 1991, the Lord inspired me to start a support group for women named **Mothers In Crisis**. I asked a group of women who were a part of the support groups that I had run in the past if they would like to be a part of **Mothers**

In Crisis and many said that they would. We started a weekly support group meeting in my small two-bed room duplex. I knew transportation had to be provided in order for the program to be successful so we picked the women up in our cars. Childcare was another barrier; therefore we provided babysitting services for the mothers who needed to bring their children. The long-term vision for **Mothers In Crisis** is to become a national organization with chapters all over the nation.

Those were the days. I had four years clean and Janar was only three years old. I had remained drug-free up until that point in my life but deep inside I knew that I needed additional support in order to continue. I was attending church but I needed more in the way of specific support centered on issues related to drug and alcohol addiction. I could not relate to the Narcotics Anonymous support groups that were available at the time. They discouraged participants from talking from a religious perspective in relation to their recovery. They encouraged everyone to use the term "higher power" when talking about God as you understood him to be. Subsequently, God could be the group, a tree, or whatever. As a black woman whose roots were firmly planted in the soil of the African Methodist Episcopal Church that I grew up attending, I could not reduce my relationship with Jesus to a "higher power." I simply didn't fit in. Therefore, the motivation for starting **Mothers In Crisis** initially was to insure that I would continue to live a drug-free life. I needed the support. I received it through the creation of a model of intervention and support that was gender and culturally specific.

In 1993, in order to receive additional education and information, I attended a week-long intensive training in Boston, Massachusetts at the *Casper Treatment Program for Women*. It was there that I learned about the relational model of intervention. The basis for the relational model is the premise that women are primarily relationship oriented and that addiction causes major disconnects in the relationships of women and their families, significant others, and especially their children. The whole focus of intervention then becomes to help women bridge the gap and create healthy relationships. Since statistics proved that women flourished in environments that adhered to the relational model, I decided to utilize this particular concept in the creation of **Mothers In Crisis** support services.

Mothers In Crisis did not start out as a grant funded program and we vowed to not base our existence on grants. I had worked in the field long enough to see that often when the grant money ended so did the program.

Therefore, **Mothers In Crisis** is primarily a volunteer driven movement that is not dependent upon grant money to survive. We vowed to continue with or without grant support because **Mothers In Crisis** is an organism, alive and growing. Over the years I have really learned to value that principle. If all of the grant money went away, we would still exist, helping families in crisis. **Mothers In Crisis** was faith-based before it was acceptable or popular to be so. It has taken a lot of faith to continue year after year. Our faith is what keeps us going during the lean and mean times!

The **Mothers In Crisis** headquarters is

located in a two-story house in the heart of a very impoverished community in the City of Tallahassee. According to a community assessment survey conducted in December 2002 (Providence Community Action Survey Report), the population of the neighborhood is predominately black, with African-Americans comprising 87% of the neighborhood. Approximately 59% of the population is children and young adults under the age of 24 and 66% of the families with children are single-parent households. The unemployment rate in the neighborhood is 20% versus 6% for the City of Tallahassee. The percentage of families living below the poverty line is three times that of the City. Only 7% of the residents in the neighborhood are homeowners. There is also a high percentage of drug use and crime occurring in the neighborhood because of its transient nature. **Mothers In Crisis** couldn't be located in a better place in order to impact a community in need.

Following is a list of services offered through **Mothers In Crisis**.

➢ **Kids In Partnership (KIP)** is a comprehensive community-based tobacco, alcohol, drug, and violence prevention program for children between the ages of 5-12, whose parents are overcoming obstacles such as drug and alcohol addiction, domestic violence, poverty, etc.

KIP evolved out of the babysitting services that were provided for the women. One day it dawned on us that if we didn't begin to work with our children they could very well repeat the cycle of addiction.

➤ **Parents In Partnership (PIP)** is a community-based parenting program that provides parenting classes, support groups, and referral services to at-risk families. **PIP** was primarily established to help families who had lost their children learn how to relate to and parent them upon reunification.

➤ **Teens Against Teenage Sex (TATS)** is a program designed exclusively for today's teenagers. Its sole purpose is to educate teens about how to abstain from premarital sex, drugs, alcohol, & tobacco. **TATS'** goal is to promote healthy growth and development among unmarried teens ranging from 11-18 years of age. **TATS** is the brainchild of Renae Rollins, a member of **Mothers In Crisis** who had a burning desire to help navigate teenagers through those tough teenage years.

➢ The **Mothers In Crisis Support Network (MICSN)** is comprised of women who are in recovery from alcohol and other drugs. **MICSN** provides weekly support groups for women, mentoring, and prayer. **MICSN** reaches out to families in crisis through powerful television public service announcements sharing messages such as, "Recovery is Possible," "Drugs Steal and Violence Kills," and "As Long As There Is Breath in Your Body, There Is Hope."

➢ **Men In Crisis** is comprised of men who are recovering from drug and alcohol addiction. **Men In Crisis** evolved out of the need for a support network for men in recovery. Over the years many people would ask me what I was doing about the men. If they were men in recovery, I would ask them, "What are you willing to do about the men?" Finally, a husband of a member of the **MICSN** asked if he could start a **Men In Crisis** Chapter. He had about eight years in recovery and he really liked the changes that were taking place in his wife. I asked him where he had been all of this time? The **Men In Crisis** chapter started meeting in September 2000. **Men In Crisis** support one another through individual sessions, weekly support groups, mentoring, and prayer.

➤ The **Beracha Dance Institute** was started by Alexia Jones, a mother who received her recovery through **Mothers In Crisis.** **Beracha** provides dance classes and opportunities for women of all ages to express themselves through the art of dance. **Beracha** gives hope through dance and drama.

➤ **The Single Parent Network** is a group established to support and empower single parents who live in the neighborhood surrounding the Mothers In Crisis House.

➤ **The United Services Advocates** is an advocacy group of concerned citizens united around issues related to social services.

I believe that abundant life consists of knowing your purpose and destiny in life as it unfolds. I started truly living after starting **Mothers In Crisis**. The need and desire for drugs completely left and I immersed myself into doing the will of God for my life. Everything that I had gone through began to make sense. I realized that it was all in the plan.

ABUNDANT LIFE BEGINS

THE LAST WORD

"For I know the plans I have for you, declares the Lord, plans to prosper you and not to harm you, plans to give you hope and a future."
JEREMIAH 29:10-14 (NIV)

ACT II

7

PEARLS OF WISDOM

I am embarrassed to admit that it took all of the pain and suffering that I went through in order for me to finally surrender my will and my way unto God. However, I believe that my journey to the "hell-hole of addiction" and all that came with it has helped me to come out with what I call "pearls of wisdom." Pearls are formed deep in the heart of the ocean within the shells of oysters and other mollusks as they enclose irritating foreign objects. I found my greatest treasures in darkness. It was as though I was that foreign object enclosed in the darkness of irritating circumstances. I went down deep and serendipitously found the treasures of life. I must say that I spent many years of my life "deep sea diving." I am only glad that I grabbed hold of abundant life when I did. Having experienced the darkness I can truly appreciate the light.

I am blessed to have learned many lessons from my experiences as well as the experiences of others. For the remainder of the book I will share eight powerful concepts that have tremendously impacted my life. In fact they have become an intricate part of who **I am**.

PEARLS OF WISDOM

Those "pearls of wisdom" are: the power of love, the power of prayer, the power of resilience, the power of hope, the power of unity, the power of suffering & humility, the power of passion, and the power of respect.

The names of others have been changed in order to protect confidentiality.

THE LAST WORD

"And I will give thee the treasures of darkness, and hidden riches of secret places, that thou mayest know that I, the Lord, which call thee by thy name, am the God of Israel."
ISAIAH 45:3 (KJV)

8

I AM LOVE

I've personally never met a mother who didn't love her child. However, I have met many that didn't know how to love their children because of addiction or mental illness. I have visited women in the hospital who were strung out on crack-cocaine when they went into labor. I have worked with women who have had as many as eight children, all prenatally exposed to alcohol and other drugs. I've seen women lose their children time and time again because of their addiction to various

substances. Through all of this, I have seen

women everywhere kick the habit of crack,

alcohol, and other drugs because of the love

that they have for their children. One such

mother I will call "Nicole." Nicole has six

beautiful children ages 15, 13, 11, 9, 7, and 3.

Nicole lost custody of her children during the

course of a 31-year addiction to various drugs

including marijuana, alcohol, and crack-cocaine.

Nicole first came to **Mothers In Crisis** while

she and her children were staying in a shelter

for battered women. She came to a drug

support group meeting and shared about her

addiction to crack-cocaine. She stated that she

was afraid that after she left the shelter she would return to using crack. That was the beginning of a long-term relationship with Nicole, her children and **Mothers In Crisis**. Throughout a five year period of time Nicole was released from the shelter, returned to using crack, moved from the City of Tallahassee, had a baby, went to jail, lost custody of her children and got out of jail. After going to jail she finally got serious about her recovery for almost two years. At which time she regained custody of her children only to relapse and go back to jail. However, Nicole didn't lose custody of her children when she went to jail the second time. Nicole tells everyone that the reason that she will never give up the fight is because of the love that she has for her children. Being the single mother of six children is not an easy task but love is the glue that keeps the family together.

Love was the motivating factor in my own life. The love that I had for the baby that died because of my addiction and subsequently the love that I have for my daughter, Janar, compelled me to stop using drugs and alcohol. As I carried Janar in my womb I loved her and wanted to protect her from my drug addiction. Once she was born, it was love that constrained me from going back to a twelve-year addiction. It was love that compelled me to reach back and try to help other women once I was clean. It is love that compels me to continue to share my testimony.

There is no greater force than love. I am not talking about just any kind of love, but I am talking about the God kind of unconditional love. Unconditional love is the kind of love that compelled God to send His only begotten Son into this world. Unconditional love is the love that compelled Jesus to die on the cross for our sins. That kind of love doesn't depend on what is inside of the person receiving the love but it depends on what is inside of the person giving the love. Through all of the things that I went through I finally learned how to love.

Love is unselfish and I was a very selfish person, as most addicts are. I only thought about what was in it for me. I didn't care about how my actions affected those that loved me. It wasn't until Janar came along and I had to think about someone else's welfare, that I began to be other centered and not just self-centered. Being other centered is an important part of love. I learned that I could not truly love if it was all about me. Love is an action word. If you truly love then you will lay down your life for your fellowman. I appreciated the power of love once I learned how to love. It wasn't until then that I began to realize how the love that my mother had for me had helped me in so many different ways. She loved me unconditionally and never gave up on me. It makes a big difference when you have love in your corner. That is one of the reasons that **Mothers In Crisis** is so powerful. We provide unconditional love to a group of people that are oftentimes starving for it.

Forgiveness is another important part of love. I know that sometimes when we suffer at the hands of others, we have a hard time forgiving. Forgiving is not about a feeling it is about an act of your will. I had to will myself to forgive others of past injustices. Many women that are addicted to various substances have been victims of sexual abuse. The guilt, shame, and blame that one experiences that has been sexually abused is enough to trigger addiction. Even in the case of being sexually abused as a child forgiveness needs to take place. Not so much for the sake of the abuser as it is for the sake of the abused. I was sexually abused as a child. I will share later about the impact that it had on me. Nevertheless I had to forgive. I even ended up leading the man that abused me to Christ while he was on his deathbed.

Unforgiveness hinders our ability to love freely. It hinders our ability to love God and others. Forgiveness is a very liberating experience. When we learn to forgive, we learn to love unconditionally and unselfishly. In the case of abuse, whether it is sexual, physical, emotional, verbal, etc., I am not saying that one should continue to allow the abuse to take place by any means. What I am saying is that in the heart, one needs to forgive.

THE LAST WORD

"Above all, love each other deeply, because love covers a multitude of sins."
I PETER 4:8 (NIV)

9

I PRAY

I believe in the power of prayer. I have seen God move mightily because of prayer. Prayer is so awesome because it allows you to communicate, to actually talk with God. The good thing about it is that God loves to talk to His children. I learned a secret of the universe when I learned how to pray.

Thinking back, I believe that I really learned to pray when I was pregnant with Janar. As I have shared earlier in the book, it was a very trying time for me. I was pregnant, alone, and kicking a major drug habit. For the first time in twelve years I was absolutely, positively, drug and alcohol free! It was also a very lonely time for me because I had to stay away from all of my friends and places that I used to hang out. The only thing I did was go to work and come home to an empty apartment. To top it all off, Janar's father had abandoned me in the process. I cried myself to sleep many nights and wondered why I was ever born. It was during this night season that I learned how to talk with the "Creator of the Universe" about my situation. The Lord listened as I poured out my heart to Him night after night. He comforted me and let me know that He was with me and would never leave me.

A defining moment occurred when a co-worker invited me to attend a revival with her and I accepted. I know this happened in response to the prayers that I had been praying. I hadn't been to church in years and I was seven months pregnant. When I got to the revival, the speaker of the hour, a blind evangelist, was singing, *Because He Lives*. One of the verses in the song says, "Because He lives, I can face tomorrow, because He lives all fear is gone. Because I know who holds my future, life is worth the living, just because He lives." I began to cry cleansing tears as my broken heart was filled with hope. I realized then that although I didn't know what the future would hold, I knew who held my future.

Oftentimes someone will say, "Well, all we can do is pray." Have you ever felt like that? Well, I have on many occasions especially when it came to trying to help someone break an addiction. Over the years I've learned that I can get more accomplished on my knees than trying to work things out myself. I had to learn early on that I was the only person I could change and I needed help doing that. Prayer releases God's power in a situation to go where we can't go and do what we can't do. It was through the power of prayer that God restored my mind when I had lost it time and time again. Prayer sets limits as to what the enemy can do. We find this principle in the word of God in Luke 22:31, when Jesus stated, "Simon, Simon, Satan has asked to sift you as wheat. But I have prayed for you Simon that your faith may not fail." Intercessory prayer is essential in breaking the stronghold of addiction. I thank God that I had a praying mother who, when she couldn't go and pull me off the streets, she sent her prayers, and God honored them.

I was given the vision to start **Mothers In Crisis** while praying. I was attending a conference in Columbia, South Carolina in April 1991. I was one of the panelists on a team comprised of a health department nurse and a state child welfare counselor. I was still working in the position as intervention specialist for a nonprofit drug and alcohol treatment program. During that period of my life, I used to wake up early each morning and go for a walk and pray. The first morning of the conference was no exception. I woke up before the break of day and began walking around the beautiful downtown neighborhood surrounding the hotel. I got lost. I couldn't seem to determine which way to go in order to get back to the hotel. After walking around several blocks I eventually found my way back. Needless to say, I was tired so I sat down to rest and continued the conversation I was having with the Lord. The first thing I did was to thank Him for helping me to find my way back to the hotel! As I sat there the Lord gave me the vision for **Mothers In Crisis**. I had sensed for months that there was something that I was supposed to do. On that particular day He revealed His plan for my life and that was to start a national networking ministry called **Mothers In Crisis**. At the time I wasn't even sure what a ministry was. I had four years clean and I had been going to church. I knew what church was but the word ministry was new to me. I shared the vision with a friend upon my return to Tallahassee, Florida. She enlightened me as to what a ministry was and I asked her to help me pull it together. That is how **Mothers In Crisis** began, through prayer.

Soon after receiving the vision for **Mothers In Crisis** I moved to Pensacola, Florida to take a position as an aftercare specialist. Once again I was working with pregnant and parenting women that were addicted to drugs and alcohol. I didn't forget about the vision for **Mothers In Crisis** however, and I would pray one day a week for the ministry to come forth and be successful. I used to cry out for hours on behalf of families who were in crisis because of drug and alcohol addiction. Through that experience I learned that prayer births things that are in the spirit realm, but not yet in the natural.

About a year later, the Lord instructed me to resign from my position and began the process of building the ministry of **Mothers In Crisis**. That was yet another very difficult time in my life because Janar was only four years old and I had to take care of her and myself. We were living in an apartment in Pensacola near my mother and other family members and they didn't understand what I was doing. As a matter of fact, I didn't fully understand either. I was just trusting God and following His lead. There were times when there wasn't anything but ice in my refrigerator. I prayed and fasted a lot during that year and God always provided.

To further complicate matters, I was in a relationship about to marry a man who was also in recovery from crack-cocaine. I got involved in the relationship because I was very vulnerable at the time. I was regularly attending church. That was one place that I thought that I could find relief. Not so because at the end of service one Sunday morning when I went up for prayer, the minister that had preached the message called up a man from the congregation and joined my hand in his. I had seen him at church often but I didn't even know his name. The evangelist, who was also a *prophet*, told us that God was bringing us together. Ordinarily I would have known better than to enter a relationship based upon a so-called prophecy, but because of what I was going through, I was extremely open. Therefore, I went along with the program. I eventually found out that he was still using drugs and lying. I realized that our whole relationship was built upon deception. Two weeks before the wedding I caught him in a bold faced lie about his drug use and I called off the wedding. Now that was too close for comfort!

Many times during this season I asked the Lord was it really His will for me to start **Mothers In Crisis**. I would wake up every morning before dawn and go walking along the ocean near Bay Bluffs Park. I would watch the sun rise, look at the ocean and cry out to God. Even though I was going through trials, I experienced God in very intense ways during that period of my life. I learned to lean and depend on the Lord through the trials. I wouldn't trade those times for the world!

I moved back to Tallahassee in the fall of 1992. Although the engagement to marry was off, my former fiancé moved to Tallahassee with Janar and me in hopes of getting clean so that we could start afresh. The relationship never made it but **Mothers In Crisis** did. I got a job working on a grant-funded project at Florida A&M University and I officially started support group meetings for **Mothers In Crisis** in my small two-bedroom duplex. I never stopped praying. Through the years, **Mothers In Crisis** has continued to grow through the good and bad times because of the foundation of prayer and fasting. The two go hand in hand. I always say, "If you pray, you will stay, and if you fast, you will last!"

THE LAST WORD

"Confess your faults one to another, and pray one for another, that ye may be healed. The effectual fervent prayer of a righteous man availeth much."
ST. JAMES 5:16 (KJV)

10

I AM RESILIENT

Resilience, according to *Webster's Dictionary*
means the power or ability to return to the
original form, position, etc. after being bent,
compressed, or stretched; elasticity. In a
nutshell, resiliency is the ability to bounce back.
I wish I could bottle resiliency and sell it in the
stores. I would be a millionaire. Unfortunately
resiliency can't be bought. It comes from inside
not outside. It is the survival instinct that we
are all born with turned up. I believe that

resilience can be motivated in a person or group of people who may be hopeless and feel like life is not worth living.

Over the years, I've met women that have bounced back from many horrendous situations that could have easily destroyed them, such as, being sexually abused as a child, domestic violence, rape, single parenting five or more children, living in extreme poverty, mental illness, drug addiction, etc. The key ingredient in these women's lives is resilience. One such woman I'll call "May." When I first met May, she was pregnant with her youngest daughter and very much addicted to crack-cocaine. I got the referral to go and see her and get her into treatment. May had tried to commit suicide and her family had called looking for help. This was the period in my life when I was working in the field as an intervention specialist. It was my job to do home visits, and help women to get into treatment. I'll never forget the day that I met May. She had just gotten out of the psychiatric hospital and she was in a very depressed state. She had to be about six months pregnant. I looked into May's eyes and I saw hopelessness. I asked her what she wanted and what could I do to help her? She looked at me with tears in her big brown eyes and said, "I just want to see my kids." May had three children who were in the legal custody of their father. She hadn't seen them in at least a year. She had lost custody because of her addiction. I told her that I would work with her on seeing her children if she agreed to get help for her drug problem. It was a deal. Over the course of thirteen years, I've seen May go into long-term residential treatment programs on two occasions, go to jail, go into psychiatric hospitals, and lose and regain custody of her children. May is the epitome of resilience.

It took resilience in order to go through the things that I went through and not give up. On one occasion, I was asked to speak to a sweet group of little old ladies that belonged to a church auxiliary. After I finished telling them my story and all about **Mothers In Crisis**, one

of the ladies asked me with tears in her eyes,

how in the world did I stay in school through

all of that and still finish college at Florida State

University? I looked at her and said it was the

grace of God. Later on that night I began to

think about what she asked me and I allowed

myself to go back to those days and retrieve

what I was thinking. I asked myself what was

motivating me to continue though many of my

friends had flunked out and gone back home.

Even when I did one time, I immediately got

back in by changing my major from

Communications to Social Work. I thought

about how when I lost my mind in the midst of

my mental breakdown, I went and withdrew myself from college. I thought about how I stayed in school when I got in trouble with the law and was placed on probation, and another time when I was homeless and didn't have anywhere to lay my head. I also thought about how at the height of my addiction, I would get up, go to class, take tests, and write papers. After thinking about all of these things, I asked myself why. The answer was that on a deep level education was instilled in me and no matter what I was going through, it always came back to the fact that I must graduate from college. Somehow my will had been set to graduate no matter what. Not graduating was not an option. All of my immediate family members had gone to college and they were all teachers. My mother owned a pre-school. My aunt (my mother's identical twin sister), my sister and all of my first cousins were teachers. All of my life I was told that I would go to college.

It's important what you tell your children about their destiny. If you tell them that they are not going to amount to anything in life, then nine times out of ten that's what will happen. Parents have the awesome power to speak into their children's lives whether it is negative or positive. By speak, I mean to instill values that will stick. We can't look for the school or the government or even the church to do it. We must do it ourselves. I believe as parents and leaders it is our responsibility to help set the will to achieve and overcome, not just survive, in our children and others. A true leader can inspire and motivate the resilience from within to come out time and time again. No matter how many times you fall down, get back up and try it again.

Be like that *Energizer* bunny that is "still going!"

THE LAST WORD

"For though a righteous man falls seven times, he rises again, but the wicked are brought down by calamity."
PROVERBS 24:16 (NIV)

11

I AM HOPE

Over the years I have written several public service announcements with a message of hope. I am known for saying, "Remember, as long as there is breath in your body, there is hope!" It's not just a cliché. There is power in HOPE. Hopeless people do not have a reason to get up in the morning. They think, what is the use? Living becomes mundane and meaningless if there is not a brighter day on the horizon. I felt the sting and reality of the message of hope when one of the mothers who had attended **Mothers In Crisis** took her own life. She came to **Mothers In Crisis** after seeing one of the aforementioned public service announcements. While attending the support groups for women, she mentioned how the message of hope had motivated her on several occasions as she was up late at night getting high on crack-cocaine. We felt that she needed additional help; therefore **Mothers In Crisis** referred her to a residential drug treatment program for women. She left the program prematurely and within a week she overdosed on pills. Unfortunately for her, there is no more hope of recovery, but there is hope for her family because they are still here and can pray to God for a brighter future for her child.

Hope is for the future. Faith is for right now. That is why I have faith for now, and hope for later. You can't have faith without hope because the Bible says, *"Now faith is the substance of things hoped for, the evidence of things not seen, (Hebrews 11:1, KJV)."* This is what makes hope so powerful because no matter what is happening right now, there is hope for tomorrow. In other words as the song writer Stan Vincent wrote in 1970, *"Ooh child, things are gonna get easier, ooh child, things will get brighter."* How do I know that? Because I have hope!

I have learned that no matter how dark it gets, there is light somewhere in the midst of the tunnel. I was at a conference in Orlando, Florida with my Bishop Dr. Mark Chironna when he asked us to share word pictures pertaining to our lives. I saw myself in a tunnel. It was actually a tunnel that was located in Mobile, Alabama. As I began to describe the tunnel, it brought back memories of the time in my life when I had just quit my job in order to start **Mothers In Crisis**. As I have shared earlier, it was a very trying time to say the least. I was following the vision the Lord had given me but things were not working out like I thought they would. As an outreach of

Mothers In Crisis, I began volunteering at a Christian residential drug treatment program for women located in Mobile called the **Home of Grace**. I would get up early once a week and drive from Pensacola to Mobile in order to facilitate a support group with the women. It was about 40 miles away and it took me at least an hour because of the morning traffic and the fact that the **Home of Grace** was located on the outskirts of town. I had to cross a long bridge and right after the bridge, I entered the tunnel.

As I continued to share at the conference, I realized the reason I saw myself in a tunnel at the conference was because I was experiencing a period of transition and uncertainty at that particular time in my life. I was following what I believed to be the will of God for my life, but things were looking pretty dark. As I continued to share about the tunnel, all of a sudden, I saw the lights that guided the cars through the tunnel. In the midst of the darkness there were lights to guide the way. That is what hope looks like, lights in the midst of darkness in order to guide the way. Just keep following the lights and eventually you will reach your destination.

The Bible says that we are to be the light of the world. I believe that one of the ways in which we shine is by being the light of hope that guides people through hard times. We all have times in our lives that are filled with pain and despair. The important thing is to allow our pain to give birth to hope and not hopelessness, shame, bitterness, and anger. These are a few of many negative consequences that can come out of tough times. I am glad that by the grace of God, I gave birth to hope through **Mothers In Crisis.** I was able to take all of the negative energy stored up in my life and make something positive out of it. As a result, **Mothers In Crisis** carries the light of hope in order to help others reach their full potential. Over the years, I have seen many women come to **Mothers In Crisis** who were hopelessly addicted to crack-cocaine and other drugs. I have seen them drowning in darkness only to behold the light that is provided through testimonies, love and encouragement.

The Bible says in Hebrews 6:19, "Which hope we have as an anchor for the soul, both sure and stedfast, and which entereth into that within the veil." That is truly good news because there are times in all of our lives when our souls need to be anchored and what better place than with Jesus through the power of hope.

THE LAST WORD

"And hope maketh not ashamed; because the love of God is shed abroad in our hearts by the Holy

Ghost which is given unto us."
ROMANS 5:5 (KJV)

12

I AM UNITY

Unity is a powerful force that can change people, families, communities, and nations. Together we can accomplish what we never could alone. That is why united we stand and divided we fall! I learned about true unity and teamwork through the experiences that I had establishing **Mothers In Crisis.** I had enough sense to know that in order for the organization to be successful it was going to take a group of like-minded people working together for the same goal. I couldn't do it by myself. It wasn't until three years after **Mothers In Crisis** had been in existence that the true leadership team began to emerge. I realized along the way and many women later that in order to have a powerful team, there couldn't be hidden agendas. By hidden agendas, I mean motives that are primarily selfish in nature but camouflaged to look like unity. Another issue that I had to deal with in relation to teamwork is the whole concept of "who's in charge," in other words there were oftentimes too many "chiefs" and not enough "Indians." I've learned that you cannot truly lead if you don't know how to follow. I have found that good leaders are followers who are promoted through service.

I thank God that by the power of the Holy Spirit a core group of women, whose destinies are intertwined, arose to the occasion and took their place as leaders in **Mothers In Crisis**. These women and I make up the leadership team. The team works together in order to help one another and others. True unity and singleness of mind to complete the common goal, belief in the Lord Jesus Christ, a passion to help others, commitment, honesty, and loyalty are the key ingredients that make the **Mothers In Crisis** leadership team powerful. We are united by the facts that we each received and maintain our recovery from drugs and alcohol through our personal relationship with the Lord Jesus Christ and we each have a passion to see others set free from the bondages of addiction, period—no other agenda or motives. As a result we are willing to work together through thick and thin. This has helped to keep us together in times of conflict. And believe me, there are conflicts; but it is through conflict that we grow and change if conflict is handled properly. The glue that holds the team together is the Holy Spirit; therefore the gates of hell shall not prevail against it.

I have shared much about my life. Now I

am going to share a little about the other four women that make up the leadership team, with their permission of course. The Lord called each of us to play an intricate part in fulfilling the vision of **Mothers In Crisis**.

I will begin with **Nettie Palmore**. **Nettie Mae Palmore** is a diamond in the rough. **Nettie** never meets a stranger. She is a down home woman who knows everyone in the community. Riding in the car with **Nettie** is like riding in a parade down Central Avenue. She waves at everyone she knows and some she doesn't know. **Nettie** came to **Mothers In Crisis** in 1992. I had recently moved back from Pensacola, Florida and **Mothers In Crisis** had been in existence about one year. I was in the community making a home visit in the public housing project where she lived with her husband and two children. **Nettie,** who prematurely left a residential drug treatment program and relapsed back on drugs shortly after leaving, approached me as I was going to my car. She asked me if I would help her. She knew about **Mothers In Crisis** and the work I did at the other treatment program. After finding out what was going on in her life and discerning her sincerity, I told **Nettie** about the **Mothers In Crisis** support group meetings. I told her that I would pick her up for the next meeting. We both agreed that if she couldn't get clean through **Mothers In Crisis** I would help her to get into a long-term residential treatment program.

This was not the first time that I met **Nettie**. I remembered seeing her walking the streets. One time in particular occurred when Janar and I were on our way out of town to visit my mother in Pensacola. She stopped my car and told me that she just got out of the hospital after trying to kill herself. She said she had taken so many pills until she passed out on the floor. She said that her husband saw her lying there and said, "You need to die," and walked over her. She was very hurt and had turned back to the streets when she got out of the hospital. I remember praying for her as Janar and I traveled. I didn't know it then but this was the first of many prayers prayed for **Nettie**. Now years later, here was **Nettie** telling me that she wanted help. As I looked at **Nettie**, I saw something on the inside of her longing to get out. Although she was a woman, I saw a hurting little girl.

Nettie began attending the **Mothers In Crisis** support group meetings. She would come and share her feelings and she seemed to be making progress. The only major problem was that she thought that she could still drink alcohol. The group members tried to warn her on several occasions, however, when her birthday and anniversary month rolled around, she drank some liquor in order to "celebrate." The next thing she knew, she was back walking the streets looking for a crack-cocaine rock. As Janar and I were leaving church one night I happened to see her walking down the street. She didn't look like her normal self. Her eyes were wide and she was walking extremely fast. I intimately knew that look and I soon realized that she was on a mission to get drugs. I pulled my car over and stopped her. I said, "Nettie, come on, get in the car." "Let's pray." But she said, "No, not right now," and kept walking. Once again, Janar and I prayed for her as we traveled.

Nettie stayed on the streets relapsing on crack for about two weeks. The turning point came one Saturday morning as **Mothers In Crisis** was having our monthly business meeting. We finished meeting and walked downstairs to leave only to find **Nettie** sitting down on the side of the building. **Nettie** knew about the monthly meetings because she attended several in addition to the weekly support group meetings. She looked very tired, dirty, and hungry. She said she had been there the whole time but was too ashamed to come upstairs. She also said that she heard us praying for her. We took her to get something to eat and then took her home. On the way home I asked her what happened to make her go back out there. She told me about how she got drunk during her birthday and anniversary celebration. After which, she just had to use her drug of choice, crack-cocaine. She said that it felt like the drug was calling her name and it got louder and louder the more she had to drink, until the pressure was too much to bear. I told her that I could relate to her dilemma and I asked what she learned from the whole experience. She said she finally realized that she couldn't drink alcohol! After the relapse **Nettie** was broken and began to pursue her recovery with a vengeance. She also started attending church with me and gave her heart to Jesus.

Nettie is a worshiper. She loves to praise and worship God and she doesn't care where. She is going to give God the glory.

Nettie has a servant's heart and will run night and day for the Lord just as she ran night and day chasing a high. **Nettie** brings passion to the team. I often tell her that she is a cheerleader for **Mothers In Crisis** because everywhere she goes she tells everyone about **Mothers In Crisis**. Over the years, I have watched **Nettie** and her family go through tremendous crises and have seen **Nettie's** determination to not go back to drugs and alcohol. Time and time again, I've seen her fall on the rock of her salvation instead of smoking the rock of her destruction. **Nettie** has proven herself to be a valuable member of the **Mothers In Crisis** leadership team.

Millie Poulos is the next team leader that I would like to share about. I met **Millie** at a national day of prayer that took place on the steps of City Hall in 1994. As I prayed **Millie** recognized my voice from a weekly radio program that I did on a Christian station. The show was called *Mothers In Crisis/Mothers In Christ* and the format included my testimony of being on drugs and my deliverance through the Lord Jesus Christ. She said that she couldn't wait to meet me when the program was over because she had a similar testimony. She also had clothes that she wanted to donate to **Mothers In Crisis.** I was impressed with **Millie's** personal testimony of deliverance from crack-cocaine, alcohol, and other drugs. I asked her to come and share with **Mothers In Crisis** at our next business meeting.

I will always remember the day **Millie** came to the business meeting. We were celebrating Nettie's first year drug-free and **Millie** was our guest speaker. There was a homeless shelter located right next to the building where we were meeting. On that particular morning someone had defecated right in front of the entrance to the building. I was so embarrassed because we had "company" coming. They would have to step over the human manure in order to get into the building. I will never forget when I found out about it and began to prepare to remove it, how **Millie** took the broom and cleanser out of my hands and went downstairs and cleaned up the feces. At that moment I knew **Millie** was special and thanked God for sending her our way.

Millie's testimony really touched us. She told us that she had five years free from drugs and that she lost custody of her oldest daughter because of her use. She shared about how she and her husband had used together and how they were separated because of the drug usage. The icing on the cake was when **Millie** sang a song for us. She had such a beautiful voice that I immediately asked her to be my guest on the next radio broadcast. She agreed and that was the beginning of **Millie** becoming an intricate part of **Mothers In Crisis.** Although **Millie** had five years clean, there were still many issues that she needed to deal with concerning her recovery.

Through **Mothers In Crisis** she was able to deal with the sexual abuse that had taken place in her life at the hand of her stepfather. She was finally free enough to talk about it at the support group meetings and get inner healing. She was also able to share the hurt and pain that she went through when her oldest daughter was removed from her custody. And last, but certainly not least, **Mothers In Crisis** was there for her when she went through a painful divorce.

Over the years **Millie** has proven to be a very loyal and passionate member of the leadership team of **Mothers In Crisis**. Her love for Jesus shines through in everything that she does. She continues to sing to the Glory of God. I see **Millie** as a flower hand-picked from the Lord's garden. She continues to blossom year after year!

Alexia Louise Jones was no stranger when she came to **Mothers In Crisis** in 1994 with her four-month-old daughter. **Alexia** and I attended college together. As a matter of fact we were best friends in college and used to get high together. She moved back to Tallahassee from Atlanta, Georgia after being away for about eight years. When she first called me she had to leave a message because I was in Seattle, Washington attending a conference. I checked my answering machine upon my return home and was pleasantly surprised to hear from **Alexia.** The first thing I heard on my answering machine was, "I am saved now!" Those words were music to my ears. I thought about how in 1987 when I was pregnant with Janar and finally turned my life over to Jesus, I called Alexia and shared the good news with her. She listened but I could tell that she was not ready. I so desperately wanted her to have what I had. I wanted us to share Jesus just as we shared drugs, therefore I prayed for **Alexia** consistently over the years.

When I called **Alexia** back she said that she was staying with her boyfriend and would like for me to come see her and the baby. She also said that past mutual acquaintances told her about **Mothers In Crisis** and she wanted to become a part of it. Nettie and I went to visit **Alexia** a couple of days later. She opened the door and we hugged. When I looked into her eyes I saw fear and confusion. Her daughter was asleep in a baby carrier. She was so tiny and looked very peaceful, just like a little angel.

Alexia and I sat down and made small talk about the past. I asked her if she would like to attend the next support group meeting. She hesitated at first but then Nettie convinced her to come so we made plans to pick her up. As we prepared to leave, I could tell that Alexia really wanted help in order to make a new life for her baby, she just didn't know how. Fortunately, Nettie and I were more that willing to show her the way because we had traveled the road she was on.

Alexia began attending the support group meetings on a regular basis and she would often talk about her relationship with her boyfriend.

I AM UNITY

She was planning to marry him for the sake of her baby girl, but she didn't seem too happy about it. One day while visiting **Alexia** in her home, she was busy in her kitchen and her daughter was asleep. I was sitting at the dining room table when I asked her if she was in love with her boyfriend. She just stood there for a long period of time and didn't answer me. I could tell that the question caught her off guard and also made her think. When I realized that she couldn't answer the question, I asked her why in the world would she marry someone that she didn't love? She said that she didn't know and began to cry. I believe that was the beginning of the end of her relationship with her boyfriend. **Alexia** finally realized that she and her daughter deserved more. Her boyfriend was a drug dealer, who began leaving drugs around the house even though he knew **Alexia** was trying to stop using. **Alexia** was still drinking beer occasionally and it was only a matter of time before she picked up and used cocaine again.

Everything came to a head for **Alexia** one Wednesday night. I remember that it was on a Wednesday because I was in a home fellowship bible study when I received a call from **Alexia.** She said she and her daughter were at the Police station because she and her boyfriend had gotten into a fight. I went to the police station and picked them up and brought them to my house. I had recently moved into a three-bedroom house so I had room for her and her baby to stay with me for a while. I allowed them to stay in the biggest bedroom in my home and we named it appropriately the "recovery room."

It was during that period of time that **Alexia** truly entered recovery and began to dance. She reconnected with her source of strength through dance. You see **Alexia Jones** is a trained dancer who has been dancing since the age of seven. Her major was dance at Florida State University but because of her drug addiction she didn't complete her degree. Each day when Janar and I left, **Alexia** would go into my big living room area and dance with the Lord. Needless to say, dance was a very important part of her recovery.

Eventually **Alexia** and her daughter moved into their own place and she began working for **Mothers In Crisis**. She also went back to Florida State University and finished her degree in Dance. In 1995, she started *Beracha Dance Institute of Mothers In Crisis*. **Alexia** has proven herself to be a true friend over the many years that we have known each other. **Alexia** is a very intense gifted woman of God who I am delighted to have on the team. We were once "partners in crime" now we are "partners in

Christ!"

Last but certainly not least, I want to talk about **Renae Rollins**. **Renae** first became acquainted with **Mothers In Crisis** in 1999 after meeting Alexia at her beauty shop, *World Class Hair Salon*. She and Alexia began to talk about their common interest in working with teenagers. Alexia was working with the youth of **Mothers In Crisis** and **Renae** was just starting a program for teenagers called, *Teens Against Teen Sex* or *TATS*. In addition to being a business owner, wife, and mother of two daughters, **Renae** had a passion to reach out and help troubled teenagers because she had been a troubled youth. Her mother was a drug addict who had been using since **Renae** was very young.

Renae began attending the weekly support group meetings. She shared with us her experiences as a young girl going through turmoil because of her mother's use. She told us about the time her mother had gone to jail because she had tried to burn the house down during a psychotic episode induced by the drug known as "angel dust." She was about 13 years old and they were living in Philadelphia, Pennsylvania. After sitting in jail a while, her mother went before the judge and **Renae** was the only family member in the courtroom. The judge took pity on her mother because **Renae**

was there and released her. They had to walk
home in the bitter cold. **Renae** shared through
tears how she had taken off one of her gloves
and given it to her mother. Over time she
became angry with her mother for the many
relapses and disappointments that took place
because of her mother's addiction. As a result
she had allowed anger and bitterness to build
up in her heart. Through the support,
encouragement, and information about
addiction that she received at **Mothers In
Crisis**, she was able to forgive her mother.
Renae also shared about her own drug
addiction. She said that she started drinking
alcohol at the age of nine. She used to drink the

left over alcohol from the many parties that her mother would have. She also began smoking marijuana at a very young age. When **Renae** came to **Mothers In Crisis** she said that she had been drug and alcohol free for seven years.

Renae became an intricate part of **Mothers In Crisis.** So much so until after a support group meeting one night, she approached me in the hall and asked me if I would consider allowing *TATS* to merge with **Mothers In Crisis**. By merge, I mean that she wanted *TATS* to come under the covering of **Mothers In Crisis** and be implemented through **Mothers In Crisis**. I was totally surprised because most people that I had run into were so busy trying to do their own thing and have their own agency until they were not willing to join hands with anyone else. I realized that **Renae** knew the value of unity and teamwork. We could do more together than apart. **Renae** had a program that God had inspired her to start and **Mothers In Crisis** had access to the very teenagers that she was trying to reach. We could apply for grants on behalf of *TATS* through **Mothers In Crisis** and she wouldn't have to worry about the administrative aspect of running a non-profit agency.

Renae, who was an ordained minister when she came to **Mothers In Crisis**, has proven to be a resilient woman of God who is very creative and outspoken. Her presence on the leadership team has taken us to another level of productivity because **Renae** is a woman who gets the job done!

The **Mothers In Crisis** leadership team learned about true teamwork while going to the Gadsden Correctional Institution for Women in Gretna, Florida from 1995-1998. What started as large support group meetings for the women eventually became full fledged church services. We learned the power of unity as we each presented to the women our gifts from the Lord. Alexia would dance, Millie would sing, Nettie would testify about her recovery, and I would give motivational messages. We learned how to stick together and watch each other's back. The times that we shared at the prison were priceless. The power of God moved mightily and we saw many miracles. During that era, we met hundreds of women who benefited from what we had to offer and it inspired us to want to take the model of **Mothers In Crisis** into communities all across the nation.

The **Mothers In Crisis** leadership team is not powerful because we are all alike; as a matter of fact we are all uniquely different. The power comes when we put our differences aside and come together for the common goal of fulfilling the vision of **Mothers In Crisis**.

That vision is to see families living drug-free lives. We all have different areas of strengths and weaknesses. I have learned that we are only as strong as our weakest link so therefore as a team we must cover each other in prayer and support. It's not about competing with each other or fighting with each other, it's about coming together to fight against the enemy. Over the years, I have learned the power unity.

THE LAST WORD

"Behold, How good and pleasant it is for brethren to dwell together in unity!
PSALM 133:1 (KJV)

13

I AM HUMBLE

I am convinced that suffering is designed to produce humility. Unfortunately, suffering can also produce hardness of heart if it is not received properly. The things that I learned through suffering, I couldn't have learned any other way because of my stubborn and rebellious attitude. Addiction to drugs and alcohol is an act of rebellion that produces a mindset of selfishness. In order to break through the denial and negative thinking surrounding addiction, one must sometimes hit what is known as "bottom." A bottom is a place of suffering that in the best-case scenario produces surrender. That is not always the case because I have met many people who seem to have bottomless pits. No matter how hard they fall, they seem to have such tolerance for pain and suffering, until they continue doing things that produce more and more pain and suffering. That is the true danger in having leprosy. Leprosy is a disease that causes the inability to feel pain. Therefore those with leprosy find it hard to protect themselves from injury and loss of limbs. I've met too many people with what I call "spiritual leprosy." They have lost their ability to feel pain and have therefore lost their ability to protect themselves. As a result they experience loss of relationships, loss of jobs, loss of self-esteem, loss of mind, loss of freedom, and sometimes loss of life.

At the height of my addiction I was one of those people with a high tolerance for pain. I believe that it stemmed from my ability to self medicate and thus become numb to the pain of the sexual abuse that took place at an early age. You see I suffered sexual abuse at the hand of an uncle who was an alcoholic. It started when I was five years old. He used to bounce me up and down on his lap rubbing me against his manhood. On one occasion he even exposed his penis. I remember thinking how huge it looked and how afraid I was. I ran out of the house and down the street crying. I never told my parents or anyone what he had done because I thought it was my fault. He used to give me candy and money and then he would fondle me. I thought that because I took the gifts I was as guilty as he was. I learned much later that it didn't matter. I was a child and he was a grown man!

I didn't allow myself to tap into the feelings surrounding the violation and loss of innocence until I had lost my mind, lost my unborn child, lost the love of my life, and finally was faced with the possible loss of yet another child. It took all of that for me to finally embrace the suffering that was a part and had been a big part of my life. By embracing the suffering I allowed myself to feel the pain without medicating. I allowed myself to cry, and most importantly, I allowed myself to cry out to God. Embracing the suffering for me was to embrace the One who suffered so much at the hand of humanity. I found that through getting to know Jesus the Christ, the one who the Bible describes in the Book of Isaiah 53:3, as being ...*a man of sorrows, acquainted with grief,* I had someone who would be right there with me, relate to the pain that I was experiencing, and help me in the process. The process that I am referring to is the process of surrender.

Humility according to *Webster's Dictionary* is the modest sense of one's own importance, rank, etc. In order for me to truly surrender, I had to realize that it wasn't all about me and humble myself. I subconsciously believed that by being rebellious and using drugs, I was getting back at life for letting me down. I had to learn that even though I had been violated it didn't mean that life revolved around me. During the process of surrender I became open to listen to others. I allowed the Holy Spirit to comfort me and heal me from the violation, guilt, and shame that I felt because of the sexual abuse. Today I am free to feel. Whether the feelings are positive or negative they are mine

and I am responsible for what I do with them.

Today I can truly say that I choose to humble

myself up under the mighty hand of God

knowing that He will lift me up time and time

again. I learned that there is true power in

suffering when it leads to humility.

THE LAST WORD

"The sacrifices of God are a broken spirit: a broken and contrite heart, O God, thou wilt not despise."
PSALMS 51:17 (KJV)

14

I AM PASSION

Passionate people are people who feel deeply. In some circles expressing and talking about feelings are not accepted. We are told to think, not to feel. When you have experienced life at a very deep level of hurt, joy, pain, etc., you can't help but feel passionately because that part of you has been awakened. Drugs and alcohol numbs one's ability to feel pain, but it awakens the ability to feel passionately about getting high. So much so until you will do whatever it takes to get the drug. Therefore an addict is a very passionate person. The only problem is that the passion is misguided.

I believe that it is good to feel and express feelings. There is no compassion without passion. In order to feel others' hurt and be moved to help, one has to be in touch with one's own feelings. There is power in passion when it is directed toward a positive cause. Passion is a force that can propel you into greatness or destruction depending upon how it is expressed.

I am reminded of the account found in the Bible in chapter seven of the Gospel According to Luke that talks about the woman who washed Jesus' feet with her tears and wiped them with her hair. Jesus said that the woman loved much because she had been forgiven much. I can relate to that woman in the Bible. I know that the reason that I have given my all to the Lord and to help others is because of what God did and continues to do for me. When I was addicted to drugs and alcohol I gave it my all. I was driven to get high everyday by the addiction. My whole life was centered on drug using and drug seeking behavior. There is no way that once I am living an abundant life I am going to just sit down and not give my all to the causes that I believe in.

I have spent many passionate times with the Lord. One such time occurred in July 1985 when I created the following poem describing an experience that I will never forget.

TEARS

As I sat in my usual morning spot deep in the woods, meditating upon the Lord. I prayed for my brothers and sisters. The longer I prayed, the deeper my burden became. Gradually, tears began to roll down my face. My eyes were swollen shut as I cried in a loud voice unto the Lord. My tears engulfed me. They surrounded me in prayer. Only it was not just my tears, for it had started to rain very hard. The rain was icy cold when it hit my face and mingled with my tears. A tiny vapor of steam rose and evaporated. Hard and steady was the rain. Heavy and loud was my cry. Refreshing yet sad. Cleansing yet sorrowful was the rain as it poured.

The Lord is a compassionate God. He hears our cries and feels our hurts. He mourns when we mourn and He will lift us up and place us where He would have us to be. Trust in the Lord thy God always.

That morning the Lord and I cried for families in crises.

There are causes that need passionate people who are not intimidated by those with little or no passion. Passion moves you to do something. It is not dormant. It's like fire; it spreads. It's like water; it flows. Passion just needs a target to consume. There are people dying of AIDS everyday. There are people addicted to alcohol and other drugs. There is poverty in every city in every state and nation in the world. There are people dying who have never been loved. There are children growing up in homes with no father and in some cases no mother. There are a multitude of issues that one can expend passion towards in this life. My passion is expressed in helping hurting families. It is hard to turn passion on and off. The very thing that makes me powerful in my ability to reach out and help others is the thing that is often attacked by a system that is designed around conformity. Over the years I have faced situations where I've been told, "Don't take it personal." "Don't make any waves." Telling a passionate person such things is like saying, "Don't breath." Passion is automatic. If I kill the passion the part of me that makes me great dies.

Some people express their passion on fleshly desires and things surrounding themselves. May I suggest that we all move towards higher goals designed to not only benefit ourselves, but also help others along the way?

THE LAST WORD

"I know your deeds, that you are neither cold nor hot, I wish you were either one or the other!"
REVELATION 3:15 (NIV)

15

I AM VALUABLE

Being an addict is one of the worst experiences that anyone can face in life, especially for women. Addiction robs you of the ability to feel good about yourself because of the choices that are made in order to maintain the habit. The behavior is often so desperate in order to get the drugs, until by the time a woman enters recovery there is not low self-esteem, but no self-esteem. As stated earlier in the book, many women use drugs initially to cover-up sexual or other abuses only to be abused over and over again during active addiction. It takes unconditional love in order to recover emotionally from the scars that are opened and reopened. I am reminded of some of the women depicted in the Bible who were delivered by Jesus only to be judged by the religious system and people of that day. They weren't valued by society, but they were valued and love unconditionally by Jesus. Today there are many systems in society that do not value women, especially women who have "questionable" histories. But praise be to God, Jesus still values and loves unconditionally!

I AM VALUABLE

Once I entered recovery, in order to deal with esteem issues successfully I had to first discover who I was. I learned that my behavior did not define me. I also learned that I couldn't let people define me either. There is only One who can define me and that is the One who made me. I found my identity when I found the Lord. Through His word I was able to see how valuable I really am. I began to respect others and myself and not allow anyone to disrespect me. I have learned throughout the years that people will devalue you based upon their perceptions of your worth. Some people truly believe, "once an addict, always an addict," and will treat you accordingly. I have come to the conclusion that I will not be used, abused, and disrespected by anyone because I am a child of God and I am valuable!

I have seen many women in abusive relationships because they do not realize their self-worth. They often say things like, "I deserved to be hit, slapped, or cursed out." One of the greatest challenges lies with helping people to know that they deserve to be treated with respect and dignity at all times no matter what they have done, or are doing. God created us all equal and that is how we should treat others and how we should be treated. Remember the *Golden Rule*, "Do unto others as you would have them do unto you."

I AM VALUABLE

I have found that there are people who do not want to give credit where credit is due. They say clichés like, "Imagine what could be done if no one gets the credit." I always say, "It's not about you, it's not about me, but it is all about Jesus!" But how many of you know that God uses people? People do things for many reasons. There is some kind of payoff, whether it's money, power, prestige, recognition, or a good intrinsic feeling. That is just how we are made. Over the years, I have found that generally speaking, we expect people in the helping professions, i.e., teachers, social workers, ministers, etc., to work for little or nothing, deal with all kinds of people, and expect no recognition. After all, "It's not about you," keep on smiling and doing the work.

I have found that the only way that I can continue to work year after year, and not burn out, is by knowing that only what you do for Christ will last. And He promises and admonishes us through the Word of God in Galatians 6:9-10 (NIV), "Let us not become weary in doing good, for at the proper time we will reap a harvest if we do not give up. Therefore, as we have opportunity, let us do good to all people, especially to those who belong to the family of believers."

THE LAST WORD

"Give everyone what you owe him: If you owe taxes, pay taxes; if

revenue, then revenue; if respect, then respect; honor, then honor."
ROMANS 13:7 (NIV)

Epilogue

The "Pearls of Wisdom" identified in the book are by no means exhaustive. There are many more principles to living abundant life. The eight that I chose to talk about are the ones that have impacted my life in very deep and lasting ways. I talked a lot about the ministry of **Mothers In Crisis** in the book. I believe that is the reason my life's journey took me through some of the experiences that I have shared concerning my drug addiction and other struggles. I am convinced that the things we go through in life are to prepare us for our destiny and purpose for being here. Instead of regret for the things I suffered, I am now grateful because they helped to shape me into the person that I am today and the person I will become tomorrow. The journey is by no means over; it has actually just begun.

Testimonial

CRACK LIKE ME
By Julie Baldwin

What help is out there for people on crack? Do you know anything about that? Sure art is great and jobs are fun. Now for that I would run. But what do you do when your whole life is crack?

Crack turns you into a dirty little rat. Nobody loves, everyone runs. Start doing things you'd never had done. Lower than low, nowhere to go. Self-hatred sets in, you can't win. So sad, I'm mad, didn't even realize the beauty I'd had. The light had gone out, only darkness for me. One last cry, one last plea...GOD PLEASE HELP ME!

And so from above the master's great love, he sent me an angel. A pure white dove. She hugged me, she touched me, dirty, wretched, little me. Her love and light had set me free. She knew where I'd come from. She'd seen what I'd seen. Truth be told, she'd been what I'd been.

Her love enlightened me. Her strength encouraged me. Her knowledge did teach me.

Back on track, no looking back. Moving ever on towards what's ahead. If not for this angel, I'd probably be dead. I pray the nation her light to see. For if not for her, who would I be? I was a crack, but now I'm back with light, love and hope for eternity.

So this I beg humanity, hear my long plea, touch someone who is a shun, a rat, a wretch, a crack like me. You just may be someone's last hope for sanity. I will be eternally grateful, that fateful day Rosalind Y. Tompkins touched me.

Works Cited

Baldwin, Julie. "Crack Like Me." Unpublished
poem, 2001.

Urban and Regional Planning Dept. of Florida
State University. <u>Providence Community
Action Survey Report</u>. Dec. 2002.

Vincent, Stan. <u>Ooh Child</u>. Perf. The Five
Stairsteps. Buddah, 1970.

About the Author

Rosalind Y. Tompkins is the founder and executive director of Mothers In Crisis, Inc. (MIC). MIC, a non-profit organization founded in April 1991, is compromised of women in recovery from alcohol and other drug abuse. MIC links families and communities together to create networks of support and encouragement for families to live drug free lives.

Ms. Tompkins graduated in 1987 with a Bachelor of Science Degree in Social Work from Florida State University. She has worked in the field of women's addictions, intervention, and treatment for over fifteen years.

In addition to being the founder and executive director of MIC, Ms. Tompkins is a thrice-ordained minister. In 1998, she founded and serves as senior pastor for Turning Point International Church (TPIC). TPIC is a member of the Legacy Alliance Network of Churches under the leadership of Bishop Dr. Mark J. Chirrona.

An avid believer in community involvement, Ms. Tompkins founded the Tallahassee/Leon

County Anti-Drug Anti-Violence Alliance (ADAVA) in 1999 and the United Services Alliance in 1998. She is also active in community undertakings like the Community Neighborhood Renaissance Partnership and the Tallahassee Equity Action Ministry (TEAM), as well as Florida initiatives like Statewide Prevention Council—the Florida Youth Initiative.

Ms. Tompkins has twelve years of personal experience with drug addiction and is currently sixteen years drug and alcohol free. With both professional and personal experience with drug addiction, Ms. Tompkins believes in empowering families, who are bound to drugs and alcohol, to be all that they can be. She

often tells them that, "As long as there is breath

in your body, there is hope!"

ADDITIONAL TRAINING
- Perinatal Addiction Preceptorship at the Women's Alcoholism Program of Casper, Inc. in Boston, Massachusetts in 1993
- The University of Georgia Southeastern Conference on Alcohol and Other Drug Programs, Inc. 36th Southeastern School of Alcohol and Other Drug Studies in August 1996

ACCOMPLISHMENTS
- Founded Mothers In Crisis, April 1991
- Developed and implemented Project TRAIN in five Leon County elementary schools, 1994-2002
- Developed and implemented the Parenting Arts Project, 1996
- Wrote, directed and appeared in several high effective local public service announcements, 1995-present
- Developed and implemented the Parents in Partnership Project, 1997-present

ABOUT THE AUTHOR

- Developed and implemented the Kids in Partnership Project, 1997-present
- Established the United Southside Alliance (USA), 1998
- Founder and Senior Pastor of Turning Point International Church (TPIC), 1998-present
- Founded the Tallahassee/Leon County Anti-Drug Anti-Violence Alliance (ADAVA), 1999
- Established the United Services Advocates (USA), 2003

ACCOLADES AND AWARDS

- Named a *Tallahassee 33* Recipient in the *Tallahassee Democrat*, 2003
- Received the Florida A&M University African American Heritage President's Award, 2003
- Received the Martin Luther King Jr. Humanitarian Award from ECHO, 2002
- Received the Woman of Courage Award from Tallahassee Community College, 2001
- Received the International Who's Who of Entrepreneurs Award, 2000
- Received the Certificate of Recognition for Distinguished Leadership awards, 1995 and 1996

- Received the Florida's Finest Certificate of Appreciation and personal recognition from Gov. Lawton Chiles, 1994
- Received numerous civic and sorority organization award
- Mothers In Crisis voted Florida Alcohol and Drug Abuse Association's Organization of the Year, 2001
- Mothers In Crisis received 2nd place for the State of Florida in Intervention from the Department of Children and Families, 2001
- Mothers In Crisis featured in an *Essence* magazine article, 1994
- Mothers In Crisis featured in several local and state newspapers, journals, and publications

MOTHERS IN CRISIS, INC.

(866) 430-1050 (toll free)
(850) 222-7705 (Tallahassee FL)
(850) 580-7762 (fax)
mothersinc@aol.com
www.mothersincrisis.com

PO Box 5121
Tallahassee FL 32314

TURNING POINT INTERNATIONAL CHURCH

...where Jesus is High Priest!

(850) 350-0218

PO Box 5121
Tallahassee FL 32314

Senior Pastor
Rosalind Y. Tompkins

TPIC is a member of the Legacy Alliance Fellowship of Churches under the leadership of Bishop Dr. Mark Chironna.

Notes

Notes

Notes

Notes

Notes

Notes